Street Songs

of the

Homeless

Sandy Smith

CONTENTS

1 Second Season Shop

Second Season Shop in Saint Joseph, Missouri in the 1980s. They have from household items and clothes (The downfall is that they don't have sofas, chairs and dresses). Depending on what you are looking for. You never know what they'll have. Most items are cheap (their stuff are reasonable). You'll be amazed what you can find there. The Second Season Shop puts the effort on helping the homeless. They take donations (unwanted stuff that people doesn't want) and they sale it to help the homeless, family in need and etc. The gals there are very friendly. As long that you are looking for a certain item that they may have the answer. As long that they don't have the answer that they'll let you know where to look (to go to).

Lynn says: I like coming to the Second Season Shop to find certain things like household items, recipe boxes, decorating items and depending on what I am looking for. I tend to buy Thank You cards and other type of cards says Lynn.

Beau says: I enjoy coming here to find kitchen wear, house hold items, movies and books on repairing things.

Mr. & Mrs. Snyder says: we love coming here to find us some clothes, cards, household items, books and talk to the nice ladies here.

2 Goodwill

Goodwill opened around 1902 to 1980s. Goodwill Industries International is a nonpartisan nonprofit organization.

Goodwill in Saint Joseph, Missouri tends to have stuff that you may be looking for. They have from clothes, household items, kids' stuff and more. You never know what you could find. You never know what you might find in their store. As long that you have a Goodwill near you. Stop in and see what they may have. You might walk away with things that you may never know that they may have.

Goodwill Industries International is a nonpartisan nonprofit organization. They help those in need.

Goodwill tends to strives, enhance the dignity and quality of individuals and families by helping them to reach their full potential through education, skills training and the power of work. There are people who went through their program to have a better understanding on working and much more.

Throughout the states (where ever there is a Goodwill store) that Goodwills tends to meet the needs of all jobs seekers, that includes programs for youth, seniors, veterans and people with disabilities, criminal backgrounds and other specialized needs.

Sandy's understanding is. The items from donations and etc. tends to help those in need, she tends to donate her unused items there.

There are people who believe that Goodwill is overpriced for the things that they get for free. Sometimes you can find an item at an reasonable price. Granted that they tend to get out of hand on prices. There are people who would pay that kind of price on the item.

There are people who go to Goodwill on occasions as long that they have the money.

3 DAV Thrift Stores

DAV Thrift Stores opened in 1958 in Kansas City, Missouri at 16th and Main, since then the name has been changed to Red Racks Thrift Stores and has 12 more locations in most parts of Missouri. DAV supports the veterans. They have from clothes, house hold items and more.

There are people who likes going to DAV, they believe that they find what they are looking for and they say that their stuff are reasonable sense they have the Red Racks that they can't pass up. Most people say that DAV has amazing things that you can't pass up. That they have things that you might be looking for. That the people there are friendly and outgoing. That they are there to help you out in any way that they can. That those people who work at DAV are there to do their job. Like most people says. Don't judge the store until you go in for yourself to judge.

There are people who "DON'T" like going there, they feel like the employees are rude and disrespectful. Along with the prices being high. Knowing that there are people who does tends to go there to get items for their home, for other things. Maybe things for an rental. Depending on how you look at it.

4 Social Welfare Board

The Social Welfare Board was founded in 1913 by Dr. Daniel Morton. He established their through a Missouri State Statute. Their mission is to promote and provide the right quality mental and dental health care to help those who are uninsured poor and homeless people of the city of Saint Joseph, Missouri and the Buchanan County area.

The mission of the Social Welfare Board is to promote and provide quality health care to the underserved population residents in the City of Saint Joseph and Buchanan County in a safe, respectful compassionate manner. They are there to help in any way possible. The clinic receives funding from the City of Saint Joseph and the County of Buchanan. Additional funds are received from through donations, grants and fee for service agreements with various funding sources and the patients pay for their cost of medical and dental care. There are people throughout Buchanan County who goes there sense they are on an low income or has no health insurance. So people go there for help. Their price is right. All a person can do is contact Social Welfare Board for more details.

For more info contact them at
Phone: 816-344-5233
Fax: 816-233-5296

Their address is
904 South 10th Street Suite A
Saint Joseph, Missouri 64503
Email: info@socialwelfareboard. org

Are you in the St. Joseph and Buchanan County and need someone
to talk to along with someone to listen too? Help is only a Phone Call
Away

Child Abuse Hotline 1-800-392-3738
Rape Crisis Line 1-816-232-1225
YWCA (domestic violence help and emergency shelter) 1-816-232-4481 or 1-800-653-1477
Substance Abuse (Family Guidance) 1-816-364-1862
Mental Health Crisis Line 1-888-279-8188
Veterans Service Officer 1-816-387-2841
Shelter & Personal Care (The Crossing)
1-816-617-2148

Could go to this website for more information www.helpmenow.org

5 Lauraine

Lauraine had no one had actually believed her that she was homeless and that it got cold that night when she was on the streets. Lauraine had stolen food from stores, at that time she was in Kansas City, Missouri pregnant and she really believe that God is the one know how help her in all honesty. Lauraine got brought to Saint Joseph, Missouri and she had called left and right for a month and a half. . . and finally she got into the YWCA SHELTER and the next day I found out 2 people (families) got kicked out because one was drunk and they fought each other so she really believed that God was with her. Before the shelter she was one who lived on the streets for 3 months before she had her son right before going into the shelter. Lauraine's father helped her after she was brought to Saint Joseph, Missouri that is where she was for 2 weeks. Lauraine is still learning things to this day. She is thankful for all the help that she's been getting from others.

Laurania is only in her twenties, still learning things on her own and getting help in any way she can. Knowing that she doesn't have much family in her life like she had wished. Laurania has been careful on what she does.

Laurania has come a long ways after being homeless; she tries her best to be a mom to her children. Lauraine has her challenges day by day. Who doesn't have those days? It's hard to be a mom, a house keeper (it's a job to clean up after every one), a wife and or girlfriend and whatever comes to day to day living these days. We gals got to do what we got to do. At least Lauraine has a roof over her head, along with her kids and her old man's head. Lauraine has issues when it comes to her children. When us gals has children. We have to protect our children. We don't want our kids to be kidnapped by others and being robbed. We know how it's like on being robbed and etc.

One day that Laurania would land on her feet by finding a good job, finding a good home and whatever that may come her way. Laurania all you got to do is keep your head up high. One day that you'll be where you want to be. Never let your dreams die. You got to look over your shoulder and keep that head up high.

6 Adam

Adam's wife kicked him out of their home. Adam and his wife has a daughter. Adam has been living on the streets. He'll stay behind the library, Hy-Vee or anywhere he can sleep. The reason why his wife kick him out. Adam was heavy on the drugs and alcohol. It torn his family apart. Sense being on the street that Adam has to figure out ways to get back on the right track. Adam has to defend himself, find food, and find money and what have you. Knowing that Adam can get the help that he needs and as long that Adam sets his mind to it.

Adam knows living on the streets isn't an easy place to be, knowing that there's killer's out there along with the drugs and alcohol and etc. Knowing that Adam has to watch what he does and to watch his back. Adam says that this isn't the life style he wants to live, that he wants to be close to his kid and people he cares about.

Like Adam says, never give up on faith, family, goals, patience, never give up on your dreams and much more. Look towards god for help and guidance and any help that you can get from others.

No matter where we are in our life. At any time that things could happen to you, our family, our friends, our neighbor's and anywhere that we could lose our house in a fire, in a flood and or god knows what. We wouldn't expect it until it happens. We tend to lose everything. To value our pictures and memories. Put them in a fire security lock box to keep it save. When we look back that we're thankful we did that. When we are out, where ever we maybe, please be nice to those who are homeless. They don't want to be treated like dirt, knowing that they went throw a lot of losing their home, their family and or everything that they had. They are no different than us; treat them with respect and the way that you want to be treated. Knowing that we had it rough at one time or another.

We all may believe that it has been an good ideal on this subject sense there are people in this world are homeless and that it needed to be more awareness on this.

These homeless people are willing to contribute to their society on where ever they are. There are programs that tends to boost their self-worth and esteem. Having to go through so much in their life that they had become a different person: leaving the homeless life behind that they have a better few of life than they had before. They can think clear, they're not on drugs and they don't drink. The help that they got, they couldn't ask for anything else. Their family couldn't believe on how much they changed. These homeless people are willing to contribute to their society on where ever they are. There are programs that tends to boost their self-worth and esteem. Having to go through so much in their life that they had become a different person: leaving the homeless life behind that they have a better few of life than they had before. They can think clear, they're not on drugs and they don't drink. The help that they got, they couldn't ask for anything else. Their family couldn't believe on how much they changed.

When we see Homeless people picking up aluminum cans, empty wet food from cats and dogs, along with tin cans that they are taking them to the recycling center to get cash. They'll even find metal and items that doesn't work to either make thing's and or get cash for them.

They'll get crafty and make things on whatever they can find. When it comes to glass jars that you'll be amazed on what they could do.

7 Phil

Phil served our country. When he got out of the services that he came out a different person. Phil settled down, got married and has a daughter. When Phil went out with his male friends, had too much to drink at a bar and rounded up at a gal's place. Phil felt bad the following day and his wife Lynda wasn't happy. Lynda told her husband to pack his stuff and get out, as Phil stayed at his parents. One day Phil left his stuff at his parents and went to Tent City, got high and got drunk. Phil really wanted to take his life back in the 1970's until Phil realized that it wasn't worth the hassle, that his daughter needed him the most. Two months later that Phil seen that girl that he spend the night at a store in Saint Joseph, Missouri. The girl told him that she was having a baby and it was his. Phil felt bad for getting her pregnant. His wife Lynda filed for a divorce. Phil lost his wife in a divorce and didn't have his family (his wife and daughter); all Phil had is his four brothers, his sister and his parents. Phil decided to go get the help that he needed. Phil got his act together after being in the VA Hospital for 2 to 4 years. All that matters to Phil is his family and his two daughters.

Phil told his oldest daughter that he still loved her mom, as his daughter didn't say anything. The look on Phil's daughter's face that she wanted to say something, instead she kept quiet. Phil's family didn't agree with him on cheating on his wife like he did. Like Phil said, we all make our mistakes and we learn from them.

Phil no matter where you are in life. You can become anything as long that you set your mind to doing it. You can find a place at the right price. Never give up. Your family and friends have faith in you.

8 Tent City

Tent City in Saint Joseph, Missouri was around since 1940 to 1950s. There were people who lost everything or whatever the reason maybe. These folks would take their tents and or buy tents from a store. They set their tents under a bridge and by the river. As people goes there that they tend to get high on drugs and to take the edge by drinking their beer. The woman felt safe there with the men. When people comes to the river to look at the view of the water along on having some fun, knowing that they don't want to deal with the homeless. Today that their not there as often. As I (Sandy) am writing this book that the stories that I've been told about "TENT CITY" that I choose not to put in this chapter about Tent City. I want to say to those of you who told me about Tent City didn't make it into this chapter.

Lisa and Gerald took food to "Tent City" for those who were hungry. Lisa is an amazing cook, her friends and family loved her cooking, her friendship and etc. The homeless people were thankful for Lisa and Gerald. Even though that Gerald is no longer in Saint Joseph, Missouri that everyone is glad to see him gone and even the people who lived around him.

When you decide to visit Saint Joseph, Missouri and see people who once was homeless or homeless to this day. Most of them would tell you all about Tent City and most wouldn't have the slightest idea what it is.

When there are people from Missouri and you tend to ask about the Missouri River, that they may tell you a story and or whatever it maybe. When I am down in the dumps and or need to get away from ever one. I like going to the Missouri River to calm myself down, along with watching the water flow and think of the good times with my dad's family and think about my late father. To this day I miss going to the river to think, to watch the river and much more.

Going to the Missouri River is so smoothing, listing to the sound of the water, those memories tends to come to you. When you do decide to go to Missouri River that you'll see how peaceful it is there. While you are there at Missouri River area (South 36 Hwy) that you can see on how the homeless people had lived. Put yourself in their place. How would that make you feel?

Plus a lot of people from Tent City tend to see animals being abandoned or abused and it tends to upset us. It's not right on what these people are doing to those animals. Those people ought to be locked up and be abused like they did to their animals, to see on how it feels like they did to their pets.

There are animals who are home; they tend to find food and water where ever they can find it. It's sad to see those animal's like that.

When we see these animals that they need a place to call home. We can take them to an animal shelter to get them their shots that they need and or for the animal shelter to find them a good home. We tend to feel bad for doing that, knowing down deep that it's a good thing to do. Knowing that they are going to a good home, those animals needed the love, the attention and etc. We hope that the people would take good care of them.

Most people doesn't realize on how bad Missouri is. Other states are getting the funding for the homeless. Where is the support for Missouri? Missouri is the last place that people think about. There are a lot of adults and children who are living on the streets. No money for themselves.

9 Losing Everything

Anonymous this couple had gone through so much. They lost their job that paid $15.00 an hour. They lost their house to a fire after paying for the house in May of 2015. Everything that they had saved went. They say that their happy that they have enough money in the bank that they had saved for ten year's. They have been sleeping anywhere they can. Liven on the streets is a rough place to be. The couple says a good place to get help is at 8th Street Community, and they'll help you in any way they can. They'll help you to get off drugs and alcohol. The couple found a place of their own. They went to Goodwill, Salvation Army and Second Season Shop to find stuff at a reasonable price. You never know what you'll be able to find. They say is to start at thrift stores until you have saved enough money. When this couple made a comment. They suggested is to save your money and let it build. Even to use coupons when you can. You can also recycle your cans and such.

Sleeping whereever isn't easy to do. We never know what a place we can go to rest. Finding a place to lay and unwind is difficult on resting our body's for the night. We tend to worry about getting run off by the home owner, the person who owns the building and or the cops. The homeless people don't have it made. They have to find a place to sleep at night. The homeless people had been known to sleep in abandoned businesses, abandoned homes, in vehicles, under bridges and whereever. When you see a homeless person please don't be disrespecting them, knowing that they aren't any different than us.

Put yourself in their spot. How would you feel that you lost your job, lost your family, lost your home and or whatever the case may be.

10 Danny Gach

Danny Gach is a Founder, a Pastor and Executive Director. Danny was born and raised in Saint Joseph, Missouri; he joined the Navy in school, served in Viet Nam as a Navy Seabee in 1969. In 1971 that Danny married his wife Twilla. Twilla worked along with Danny in various business, real estate development over the years and to this day they continue to work together at the Crossing Outreach Ministry. When most people are starting or planning beforehand on retirement, with Danny that he started The Crossing Outreach Ministry as a Pastor and opened the doors in November of 2012.

Even though that Danny tends to help folks in need, trying to engage other churches, social services, other companies and the surrounding area to come together as a community when it comes to the homeless and those who served our country.

Danny has a lot of things that he would like to see in Saint Joseph, Missouri area. With the goals that Danny has and etc. that Sandy wishes him all the best.

Knowing that Saint Joseph, Missouri could be a better place and much more. What Saint Joseph, Missouri needs is "NEW BUSINESS" (that has never been to Saint Joseph, Missouri), to have a better paying job. Along with other things.

11 Andrew County

There are people in Andrew County along with Saint Joseph, Missouri and the surrounding area in Missouri would like to see a Thrift Store called Helping Hand Store where they help the community where people are struggling financially (low income people) and those who's homeless. Knowing that it won't happen in our life time. If it does happen in our life time that it would be amazing to see. Knowing that it would be nice to see an "BRAND NEW BUILDING" instead of a rundown building like there is in Savannah, Missouri, Rosendale, Missouri, Fillmore, Missouri, and Bolckow, Missouri and around that area along with Saint Joseph, Missouri (Just Missouri itself).

12 Raising Money

Amanda is raising money to help feed the homeless people all through the United States and other countries and Amanda could use your help. When she reaches her goal that her plans on buying a bunch of food, water and etc. and donating it to the homeless shelter all over. To donate go to https://www.gofundme.com/9mezd-homeless-family&rcid=r01-153017173803-975686e5827d462b&pc=ot_co_campmgmt_mand help Amanda out.

There are homeless people who would tell you that it's not an easy on being homeless, that you are being judged on sleeping where ever. Those who "AREN'T HOMELESS" are lucky to have a place to call home.

13 Heather

Heather Duncan - Sullivan is the person and the voice for the She Does movement in Los Angeles area. Heather was once experienced "HOMELESS". Heather too fell victim to sexual abuse while living on the streets in Santa Monica. At the time that there was no justice for her. Heather is a Homeless advocate for the Homeless woman and children. Heather is speaking up against the abuse and violence on her streets each and every day and night. Join them in this fight to end the above save their woman. Heather has been working as a Homeless Advocate for the homeless family. Heather understands what the homeless are facing and going through since Heather had experienced homelessness herself.

Heather is very compassionate and dedicated to helping families there in her area. Heather has been very blessed to have an amazing family and friends who has supported her "Homeless Organization". Heather's mission is to end homeless and hunger in one heart one soul and one community at a time.

Heather isn't just another pretty face. She is the face and the voice for the She Does movement in Los Angeles! Heather once experienced Homelessness and Heather too fell victim to sexual abuse while living on the streets in Santa Monica a little over 13 years ago! There was no justice for Heather what so now at 43 and a Homeless advocate for Homeless woman and children. Heather is speaking up against the abuse and violence on her beautiful streets each and every day and night! Join us in this fight to end the above and save our Woman!!!

Heather had personally experienced firsthand and it took her 4 very long painful years to be able to pick herself back up and very life back on track! Heather never asked to be Homeless nor did she ever think she would end up Homeless; she actually was forced into this situation by her own family over 13 years ago. Her story is about survival courage and inspiration and when she first become Homeless in Los Angeles that she had no clue where to look and find help Heather felt all alone scared frighten and terrified being a single mother and a women! Friends and family helped her out by putting her in hotels money for food and Heather, I lived in and out of motels and hotels for a while and then I was able to find cold weather shelters and then she got a 6 month bed at a shelter in Santa Monica!

Once Heather got into a 6 month shelter Heather was able to work and put herself through school at SMC Heather become a music major and graduated with a smile on her face and with great pride!

During Heather's four years of being Homelessness that she also at one point received services through O. P. C. C access center, Saint Joseph's access center, Chrysalis Catholic Charities, Step up on

Second, Edelman Mental Health just to name a few places that had a major role in life!

There were times Heather ever slept on the beach or in parking lots or even her car and believe Heather it was not easy nor fun it was extremely difficult for her and hard on her body mind and soul! One night Heather's husband and I even got caught up in a Homeless sweep on the middle of the night during a rain storm by the Santa Monica police department just because we were Homeless! Thank God that case was thrown out of court a few months later!

William stands by his wife Heather's side, with all the choices that Heather makes that William is there. When Heather has an ideal that she tends to let me in on what's on her mind and I tend to think about it and I let her know what I think. That's what makes a perfect marriage. I William knows how it feels on being homeless. I once was homeless, it wasn't an easy life than. There would been people a talking, they would never know on how it feels until they experience it themselves on how it feels on being homeless. Why can't they put their selves in our predicament and see on how we feel on being homeless. I am thankful that I meet my beautiful and amazing wife. I tend to help my wife make jewelry to help my wife. I believe that we make a good team.

Homeless tends to affect millions of Americans every day, it could happen to you and it could happen to me. Let's work on this together to help the "HOMELESS" and provide more shelters with transitional housing, that way they'll have affordable housing that is the key ending to homelessness.

14 Lisa

Lisa lived in Portland, Oregon with a couple till the couple lost their home, Lisa stayed in friends vehicles and anywhere she could sleep. It was rough for Lisa, the good thing is though, she was working as an volunteer at Second Harvest pantry. Lisa really enjoyed it there until she made a choice to move from Portland, Oregon to the California area to work. Lisa couldn't be happier and that she doesn't have to be out on the streets doesn't have to sleep in vehicles and where ever.

Lisa looks at life in a different way now, having a better life style that she couldn't ask for a better life. Lisa is happy, thankful, enjoys life and etc. Has a home where she can be home, along with someone to be happy with and so forth.

Today those who had either gotten a place of their own, gotten help from a family or friend, gotten help from an case worker and or whatever resource it maybe to get the homeless off the streets. Whatever their story maybe that it'll take time to recover from being homeless. Being out there is rough, always watching over their backs and etc.

Lisa is in a place in her life where she feels safer. Lisa found someone in her life and couldn't ask for anything better. Lisa is staying strong and living life to the fullest.

15 Homeless in California

There are many people in California area are alarmed with the increasing the number of people who are putting up tents on sidewalks, under freeways in the city, behind businesses, and behind family and friends places to camp out. They never asked to be homeless, knowing that they are the ones who lost everything.

Even though there's a lot of vacant properties that hadn't been used in years. As the city and the community ought to come together and take a look at the vacant public and private lands on how they could use it for. There are people who would like to see homeless shelters.

In today's world that the homeless individuals has been sleeping on benches, doorways, sidewalks, under freeways and other places to sleeps are common sights in major cities up and down the states.

16 Help the Children

We tend to see these children roam around on the streets without their parents. Some times that these kids tend to run away, that they are being abused by their parents and or their parents are using and or drinking. We never know their story. These children maybe homeless, lost and or whatever their story maybe. Today's world that these children parents deceased doesn't have a place to call home. It's sad to see these kids go homeless. We tend to think of ways to help these children out in any way that we could. We tend to see these commercials and we tend to think on how we could contact them to get their help. To help these children out in any way we can. Place them in our care until we could get more info on getting these kids off the streets. Be brave, be kind, be loving and caring and step up to help these children. Anything that we can do to help these children.

We tend to think of Children's Fund and other organizations.

The Children's Fund opened in 1985. The Children's Fund tends to help the children who are at high risk and who fell under the responsibility. They tend to help those children who needs help and or whatever the reason it is. For more info contact https: //www.childrensfund.org/

Here's a second one that's called Kiwanis Children's Fund

At Kiwanians Children's Fund that they tend to help change these kids' lives around and they often in ways that would otherwise remain beyond the resources of clubs and districts. You would be surprised on what they do there at Kiwanians Children's Fund. For more info contact http: //www2.kiwanis.org/childrensfund.

Support your favorite organizations on helping the children in need.

Knowing that we were children once and got supported from other's at one point or another.

No matter where you are at. Could you help the children in need?

17 Ryan and Crystal

Ryan Holets, a cop in Albuquerque, New Mexico. Officer got a call and encountered two people struggling with addiction to heroin, Ryan saw Crystal off to a side behind a gas station. Ryan got was 7 to 8 months pregnant and living on the streets, as Crystal was shooting up drugs that it made Ryan to his thoughts, as he shut off his body cam and collect his thoughts. That's when he knew his wife would be up to it, as Ryan talked to his wife that they were going to adopt the baby.

As Ryan got Crystal the help that she needs. Crystal knew what she was doing to her baby is harmful. As Crystal got herself cleaned, that she's trying so hard to chance her life around. Crystal is thankful for the help Ryan had done for her.

There are law enforcement throughout the states tends to help out. Like in Ryan's case that he step to the plate and be the man as he is and thought that Ryan and his wife to adopt the baby. There are nice law enforcement's that would tend to help in any way he or she could help in any way possible. Thankfully that Ryan was in the right area at the right time. Even though Ryan and his wife Rebecca already has 4 children of their own.

Ryan and Heather opened their home to Crime Watch Daily, sharing the details of what happened. It aired on 2/8/2018 and on 7/19/2018.

When we see law enforcements out thank them for everything they do. We may not like most of them. Knowing that they are there to keep our streets safe.

18 Abuse

Abuse
No matter what if we are homeless or not homeless and when we
tend to go out in public that we tend to see couple fight (who doesn't
argue?), when a person takes their frustration out and he or she tends
to abuse that person step in and break it up. There are times that we
don't want to get involved. We got to do what's best by report it to
the cops.

DON'T BE SCARED OF SPEAKING UP. SPEAK UP AND LET
YOUR VOICE BE HEARD. YOU DON'T HAVE TO BE
ABUSED, SEXUAL ABUSE AND OTHER TYPE OF ABUSE.
YOU NEVER KNOW THAT YOUR VOICE MAY BE HEARD.
NEVER BE AFRAID TO PUT YOUR STORY OUT. THERE
ARE PEOPLE WHO ARE LISTENING.

The reason why some people are homeless is because they have
nowhere to go when they leave an abusive relationship sense they

were being abused and don't want to be in that abusive relationship.

When we were younger that we had DREAMS for ourselves. We couldn't wait till we moved out of our parents and or single parent homes. Our dream was either to go to college to become something, finding a good paying job, finding a good home and or whatever that comes our way until everything went downhill that lead us to homeless, jail and or prison. That our DREAMS had failed.

19 Money

There are people who wonder how the homeless make money. The homeless people tend to find money on the ground, collect cans, scrap metal and etc. to take to the recycling center to make money. Even the homeless people tends to sell items.

They are struggling on money as well. Knowing that they have to work for their money and other ways to make money. No matter if we're homeless or not homeless . . . that there are people throughout United States are struggling. Those who has a good paying job doesn't tend to struggle like most of those who are getting $7.00 an hour and under on an paying job and those who are on disability who are the ones who are struggling the most. Those who aren't working are the ones has to do what he or she has to do. Those who are struggling financially tends to figure out ways to bring in extra money.

There are people who tends to take the time to collect aluminum cans, tin cans, glass jars and etc. to take them to the recycling center. Most states don't take glass jars and plastic to make extra money.

Truthfully there are people in Missouri who collects glass jars tends to resale them to make like extra money. You never know what people could do with glass jars.

20 Donald Trump

We don't know if you had noticed that there are homeless people throughout the United States. What are you going to do to make the homeless stop? There are more and more going homeless. They had either lost everything by a fire, water and whatever it maybe. These homeless people has to do what they have to do to take support themselves, their family and etc.

SO MR. TRUMP, WHAT ARE YOU GOING TO DO TO HELP THE HOMELESS. GET YOUR HEAD WRAPPED AROUND THE HOMELESS PEOPLE AND BRING IN GOOD PAYING JOBS IN SAINT JOSEPH, MISSOURI AND IN ANDREW COUNTY AREA.

Most people don't know about you. These people believes that you aren't doing what you are supposed to do. What happened on doing the things you wanted to do Donald Trump? Everyone believes that you are the worst president. People who voted for you believe that you are doing an amazing job. They believe on having those unwanted people who shouldn't be in our country that they ought to go back where they came from. Mr. President Donald Trump, these people wants to see things being done.

Why don't you get an hair cut?

Donald Trump what would you do when there are so many people cannot text and drive because too many accidents of innocent people are happening? Knowing that there has been so many accidents with people texting and driving and even people talking on their cell phones. The cops are the worst when it comes to the cell phones.

21 Doug the Bounty Hunter

When Sandy is out and about that she hears the Homeless people talk about Dog the Bounty Hunter (Duane Chapman) and his wife Beth. How they wish that they would come to Saint Joseph, Missouri and the surrounding area to get the streets cleaned by getting rid of the drug users, alcoholic's and the abusers off the streets. Missouri needs a safe place without worrying about the drugs in our neighborhood (where ever we live at). It's not safe where ever we are. There are people who lives on the streets who would kidnap a child and women. Depending who you are (even some woman who kidnap a guy). Some women tend to not be in their right mind. We (kids, women and men) have to be careful.

Sandy believes having Dog the Bounty Hunter & Beth here in Saint Joseph, Mo would help teach them from right to wrong. Sandy sees too much in her lifetime. Sandy knows how it feels when it comes to alcohol sense Sandy had few family members who had drank. Sandy thought on having Dog the Bounty Hunter here in Missouri that it would help those who abuses drugs and etc. to get them the help that they need.

Duane "Dog" & Beth Chapman has helped so many people when they had caught the people who had jumped bail, abused drugs and whatever the case might be.

22 Sandy's Dream

Sandy had a dream on opening an homeless shelter. Knowing that it takes money. Sandy's dream fail through since she's always broke. One thing about Sandy though. Sandy tends to help others out when they need her help. She's not lazy like most people puts her out to be. The people that are close to her would tell you that Sandy is a very hard worker and she tends to get it done. When Sandy has her mind on doing something that she gets in there and gets it done. Watch out folks. You really don't want to be in her way. Sandy hates people getting in her way. Sandy is the most respectful, caring, honest and an hard worker.

Sandy tends to see Homeless people everywhere, she wishes that there would be more shelter's and people would bring the Homeless people in during the "HOT AND COLD DAY'S". Sandy knows there are people who really doesn't want the "HOMELESS PEOPLE" in their home, sense we never know what they'll do (they can kill you and rape you). We can't trust anybody.

23 People Who Are Different

There are Bisexual, Gay and Lesbians that are homeless for god knows why. They tend to get made fun of because of what they are, truthfully to be honest that they aren't any different than any of us straight people. We all do things different, knowing that things gets done.

There are people who asks these questions.
1. Do they work like a straight person?
Yes they do. They tend to work hard to make a life for themselves.
2. Do they want kids?
There are some who wants kids and some don't. Depending on the couple/person.
3. Does their family approve of their lifestyle?
Most of their family knew that they were like that. Most of the family doesn't approve. The thing is, is that their isn't nothing that the parents, siblings and the family can do. Our kids are going to do what they want to do. We wish that they wouldn't make that choice.
4. How do they save money?
It's not easy on saving money. They tend to put it where it'll be saved.

It can be at an relative's place and or at a bank. It all depends.

5. How do they bathe?

That's a good question. They may have friends that they may know would let them take a bath or shower. Maybe an homeless shelter.

6. Do they get crafty?

Yes they do. They tend to get crafty in a lot of ways. Once they get enough they tend to sell them to make money from them.

7. Do they recycle?

There are some who does. There are people tends to save them for them to help them out.

When you are in a big city such as Kansas City, Missouri, Saint Louis, Missouri and California tends to have major disasters. Their homes could get flooded or destroyed in their neighborhood and has to evacuated. In certain situations that there are emergency shelters would take people in.

Trying to cook food is difficult to do while being homeless. It's different from cooking in everyday life. The homeless people would have portable grills, tends to use the grills at the park and other ways to cook.

24 Educate Yourself

As long that you are one of the lucky ones that you are grateful, the world of a homeless person is completely different than your own, without the support from our family and friends, just how many of them could survive something such as loss of a spouse, physical illness and or the loss of employment?

All we can do is educate ourselves. There are reasons why a person becomes homeless, the lack of affordable housing, loss of a job, a divorce, illness, substance abuse and cetera. One of the first and most that you can take towards helping the homeless is to understand on how they got there in the first place and how we can help.

Show Some Respect: When we are around homeless people, don't treat them as if they were invisible. You could strike up a conversation on a bench or where ever you maybe.

Volunteer: There are places that you can go and sign up to work at your local homeless shelter by answering phones, sort out mail, serve food, wash dishes, laundry and whatever that needs to be done.

Teach: You could always put your skills in good use by sharing them with the homeless, along by organize an class through your local shelter. Those skills can help a homeless person find work and to become a person.

25 Tabitha

Tabitha Painter's 42nd birthday was coming up on September 21st and thought about opening an homeless shelter for single woman and woman with children. Tabatha thought of a name Ilene Rose Shelter, the name Tabatha came up with is names of her Grandma's middle name and Great Grandma's name and that they were victims of abuse from their spouse and that they had to get out of the home with their children to keep them safe. Tabatha had cameras on her building in the inside and out with police officer's on the property to keep the gals and children and the gals who stayed with their children felt safe. They wouldn't know what to do without Tabatha. Tabatha had seen a lot of abuse, drugs and much more, that's when she step up to be the voice of the victims.

Tabatha has seen to many people going homeless or are homeless. What saddens Tabatha is she see's parents with babies and young children. It saddens her to see people go homeless.

Tabatha is happy to have parents like here's, she couldn't ask for better parents. The thing is, Tabatha didn't know that her parents were homeless back in the late 1960's early 1970's, that her parents told her on what was like. Her parents told her that they meet Charles Manson and his people before they got locked up, that they (Tabatha's parents) had more people around to keep them safe. Tabatha had heard about Charles Manson.

Today as Tabatha has the homeless shelter open that there are 100 to 150 people are in her shelter safe, along with people bringing in food, snacks, water and what have you to help out the shelter. There has been people who had mailed Tabatha money to use towards the shelter.

Tabatha had done a lot of resources from family, friends and co-workers for the woman, she seen abuse with her aunts, cousins, friends and co-workers. Tabatha talked to a couple who are Catholic's for advice to open an woman's shelter for single woman and woman with children, as Tabatha took notes that she put her notes into an folder to look over to memorize them and she's thankful to learn from her pastor. Her pastor is a school teacher and a counselor, Tabatha looks up to her as a room model. Tabatha recommends them to anyone who needs counseling to deal with their abuse. Tabatha would help them with job training sense her mom taught her skills on how to sew, farming, stocking shelfs, budgeting money, along with other things that they ought to learn so that they could live on their own at some point and with a better life.

Tabatha had learned so much over the years and thankful for everything that people had taught her. Tabatha learned from the best. One day unexpected that her pastor called her up where they were, there were six families who were sitting in the front who she meant the most to, with the City Council and with a few City and State Cops were there and rewarded her with $20. 000. 00 with clothes, diapers, toys and etc. Tabatha wasn't expecting it when she got recognized by the town of Liberty, Missouri for her charity work.

These woman are thankful to have Tabatha, they admire what she does and they look at Tabatha as a mentor. They are thankful to have an amazing gal like Tabatha.

In Tabatha's mind that she could find a crew who could build cabins like the ones like at Camp Rainbow in Trenton, Missouri to put on her land. Knowing that others would love it as much as Tabatha and others has when they went to Camp Rainbow.

26 Aaron

Aaron was born homeless and not proud to be homeless. Aaron has all these dreams that he wants to do since he was little. Aaron's uncle is the oldest Metis Veteran in the country and was awarded medals and he is the first in his immediate family to finish University. Aaron's father is schizophrenic; mother is bipolar and had abandoned them before Aaron was born, she wasn't capable of raising Aaron, she was very abusive, mentally and physically, one of her boyfriends was involved in sexually assaulting her and Aaron. The courts were involved in Aaron's entire childhood, as he was in and out of children's aid.

When Aaron turned 14 that the police arrested Aaron's mother again, later another judge changed Aaron's guardianship to no one. Aaron had lived with his girlfriend until her mother (who was also poor) could no longer support Aaron. Aaron finished that year of school sleeping in the park and he is the first in his immediate family to finish University.

STREET SONGS OF THE HOMELESS

ABOUT THE AUTHOR

Sandy Smith lives in St. Joseph, Missouri, where she is very interested in trying to help out the homeless, wherever they are.

Made in the USA
Monee, IL
27 January 2020